Camp Lewis: Tacoma, Washington

Belmore Browne

In the interest of creating a more extensive selection of rare historical book reprints, we have chosen to reproduce this title even though it may possibly have occasional imperfections such as missing and blurred pages, missing text, poor pictures, markings, dark backgrounds and other reproduction issues beyond our control. Because this work is culturally important, we have made it available as a part of our commitment to protecting, preserving and promoting the world's literature. Thank you for your understanding.

CAMP LEWIS

TACOMA WN.

Compiled by
BELMORE BROWNE

Press of
COMMERCIAL BINDERY & PRINTING CO.
TACOMA

Copyrighted, 1918

CAMP LEWIS

A HISTORY OF THE DEVELOPMENT OF THE LARGEST PERMANENT MILITARY CANTONMENT IN THE UNITED STATES

Stretching southward from the City of Tacoma in the State of Washington, lies an upland region of great beauty. It is formed by an ancient glacial shelf that lies between the blue, forested foothills of the ice-clad Cascade Range and the clear, cold waters of Puget Sound. It is a land of quiet lakes and sparkling streams, of grassy and evergreen trees—a natural park where Nature has worked unhampered and produced a region of sylvan loveliness.

In the early days Fort Steilacoom on the north and the old Nisqually trading post on the south were the nearest settlements and it was called the Nisqually Plain after the Indians of that tribe who herded their horses on its green pastures.

With the passing of the pioneer days and the coming of the railroads a new era dawned for the Northwest, but the cities sprang up at tide water and the farmers settled the more fertile valleys and "the prairies,' as the newcomers called the rolling uplands, were left to themselves. This enforced isolation continued for a number of years, but as the methods of transportation improved, the splendid natural roads of the region were worn smooth by the wheels of bicycles and automobiles and "the prairie" became a vast pleasure ground.

Before the prairies came into their own, however, the military advantages of the region had been demonstrated when the first organization of State troops chose the shores of American Lake as the site for their summer encampment. Every time they were used the regulars participated. On that instant was born the plan that through years of effort on the part of far-sighted men has developed into the largest military cantonment in the United States.

In October, 1916, Major General J. Franklin Bell, Commander of the Western Department of the U. S. Army, sent Captain Richard Park to the Northwest to investigate sites for an army post. Through some oversight the American Lake site was not included in Captain Park's list, but the fact that he was engaged on such a mission became known to Stephen Appleby, Cashier of the National Bank of Tacoma, who was attending the business men's military encampment at American Lake. Mr. Appleby got in touch with Captain Park, who in company with Colonel U. G. Alexander, Commander of the business men's camp, Major Logan and Mr. Jesse O. Thomas, inspected the site. On receipt of their favorable report, Major General Bell visited the site and before a meeting of prominent business men he added his enthusiastic endorsement to the plan and called attention to the fact that in August, the U. S. Senate had passed a military bill which included the clause which allowed the Secretary of War to accept, as donations, such sites as were adapted to military purposes.

Here was the opportunity which had been so eagerly desired by the far-sighted men of the community and without a moment's hesitation it was accepted. A fund was instantly raised by popular subscription and Mr. Appleby went to San Francisco where he obtained a definite recommendation of the site from Major General Bell. On the 15th of October, a Committee composed of Mr. Appleby, Mr. Frank Baker and Mr. Jesse O. Thomas, went to Washington, D. C., where they were joined by Mr. Elbert H. Baker, of Cleveland, Ohio. They were received by Secretary of War Baker, and the entire matter was studied with the utmost thoroughness. Mr. Applby's Committee was authorized to offer to the United States Government a tract of one hundred and forty square miles, of which 108.2 sqare miles, or approximately 70,000 acres, was to be acquired under condemnation procedings on the understanding that the Government would establish thereon a permanent military mobilization, training and supply station. The land was selected by Major General Bell. No private citizen had any hand in it. Speculators received no consideration when the proposition was initiated, nor during the subsequent procedings. The prices were to be fixed by jury.

After studying every phase of the proposal in company with Major General Bell, Major General Hugh L. Scott and other army heads, the Secretary of War signified his willingness to sign an agreement binding the United States Government to assign a division of troops to the American Lake site. Before giving his final consent, however, the Secretary consulted the President. The matter was of such importance that President Wilson did not wish to assume full responsibility for the step, and as he was at that time in the concluding part of his campaign, a wait of several weeks was necessary. With the election over, he found time to study the matter, and after Senator Chamberlain, Chairman of the Senate Military Affairs Committee, and Congressman Dent, Chairman of the House Committee, had approved of the project, the President added his endorsement.

Up to this time a considerable part of the Tacoma public had remained luke-warm towards the project, but the conference in Washington, D. C., resulted in a letter from the Secretary of War definitely approving of the proposed gift.

The question of whether or not the American Lake site was to become a national military reservation was now squarely "up" to the citizens of Pierce County, and that they appreciated the national and local importance of the project was shown by the energy and spirit with which they went to work. On December 4th, 1916, Mayor A. V. Fawcett, of Tacoma, issued a public proclamation stating that the Government had accepted the site. On the same day a commitee of one hundred and fifty of the leading business men presented a petition to the Board of County Commissioners, requesting them to call a bond election for the purpose of obtaining the assent of the electors of Pierce County to the borrowing of a sum of $2,000,000.00 and the issue of bonds of the County therefor, for the purpose of purchasing and presenting to the Government the American Lake site.

The petition received the enthusiastic support not only of the Board of County Commissioners composed of J. W. Slayden, W. H. Reed and C. H. Williams, but also of the two county commissioners-elect: T. H. Bellingham and James R. O'Farrell who were present.

The election was called immediately, and January 6th, 1916, was the date set by the County Commissioners as the date for the holding of a special bond election for the purpose of learning the will of the people.

At the same meeting the County Commissioners engaged J. T. S. Lyle as special attorney to have charge of all legal work in connection with the bonds and the condemnation proceedings.

Once begun, the civic drive never ceased. Meetings were scheduled for every town and hamlet in Pierce County. An Army Post headquarters was established and an army of Tacoma men and women offered their services free. Election officials who served during the presidential contest for a goodly stipend came forward and offered their time and energy gratis as guardians of the polls. Associations, clubs, societies, orders, labor unions and individuals vied with each other in carrying on the good work. The property owners of the land in question fell into line at once. Step by step, and point by point, the project was eagerly and comprehensively detailed to the voting public; and, as the campaign was nearing an end, Major General Bell added the force of his vast experience and personal strength to the great drive.

The election was held on the appointed day and ended in an overwhelming vote in favor of the post. The total vote cast numbered 29,199, and of these 25,049, or about 86 per cent., were in favor of the great project.

It is impossible at this time to grasp the full significance of this magnificent gift to the Government by the residents of Pierce County. A new spirit is making itself manifest among the American people, a spirit that is based on the realization that we are no longer an isolted nation, but a vital part of the life of the great globe on which we live.

With our new position among the nations has come a flood of grave responsibilities. Already the principle of Democracy on which we stand has been assailed by the forces of Militarism. Every resource of our great land must be used to guarantee the spiritual freedom of mankind.

The gift of the people of Pierce County is the first contribution of its kind ever made in the history of our country, and in that fact we have just cause for pride; but there is a deeper reason for pride in the realization that back of the gift lies the spirit of loyalty and patriotism that will guarantee our final triumph over the champions of political slavery.

BUILDERS
of
CAMP LEWIS
TACOMA, WASHINGTON

LT. COL. DAVID L. STONE

LT. COL. DAVID L. STONE

Lt. Col. David L. Stone, born in Stoneville, Mississippi in 1876, entered West Point in 1894, and graduated in 1898. This class was graduated two months earlier than the usual time, and the graduates assigned to regiments taking part in General Shafter's expedition to Cuba in the war with Spain. This expedition resulted in the capture of Santiago which ended the war.

Lt. Col. Stone served with the 22nd regular infantry during the Cuban campaign and several months later went with his regiment to the Philippines where he served in the field against Aguinaldo's forces from early in 1899 to 1902, taking part in all expeditions conducted by Generals Lawton, McArthur, Wheaton, Young, Funston and Grant. After the main insurrection was suppressed, Lt. Col. Stone was assigned to command of the district and town of Cabiao, where he was engaged in constant operations against Filipinos conducting guerilla warfare. After fifteen months at home in the U. S., Lt. Col. Stone again accompanied his regiment to the Philippines, and was stationed on the Island of Mindanao, where he carried on operations against hostile Moros who are Mohammedan religious fanatics. In October, 1904, Lt. Col. Stone was wounded in action against the Sultan of Oato and was returned home for medical attention. While recovering from his wound, he was detailed on construction work in the Quartermaster Corps, on which work he has been in charge of the following construction:

Rebuilding Fort Omaha, Nebraska.

Installing electric lighting system at Fort Crook, Nebraska.

Constructing Artillery Post at Fort Sill, Oklahoma.

In charge of all construction in Hawaiian Department and building Fort Kamehameha at Pearl Harbor.

Planning and building a large post at Schofield Barracks.

Building Fort De Russy and additional work at Forts Ruger and Shafter and the mountain water system for Schofield Barracks.

From Honolulu Lt. Col. Stone returned to the U. S. in May, 1917, and was at once assigned the charge of construction work at American Lake.

This brief history of the salient events in the life of Lt. Col. David L. Stone calls our attention to two important facts: first, his devotion and many acts of service to our country; second, the confidence reposed in him by our Government.

The entrusting to his care the heavy responsibility of supervising the entire construction of Camp Lewis was, in itself, as great an honor as an American could receive, but the manner in which he has borne this responsibility has shown that he was in every way worthy of that honor.

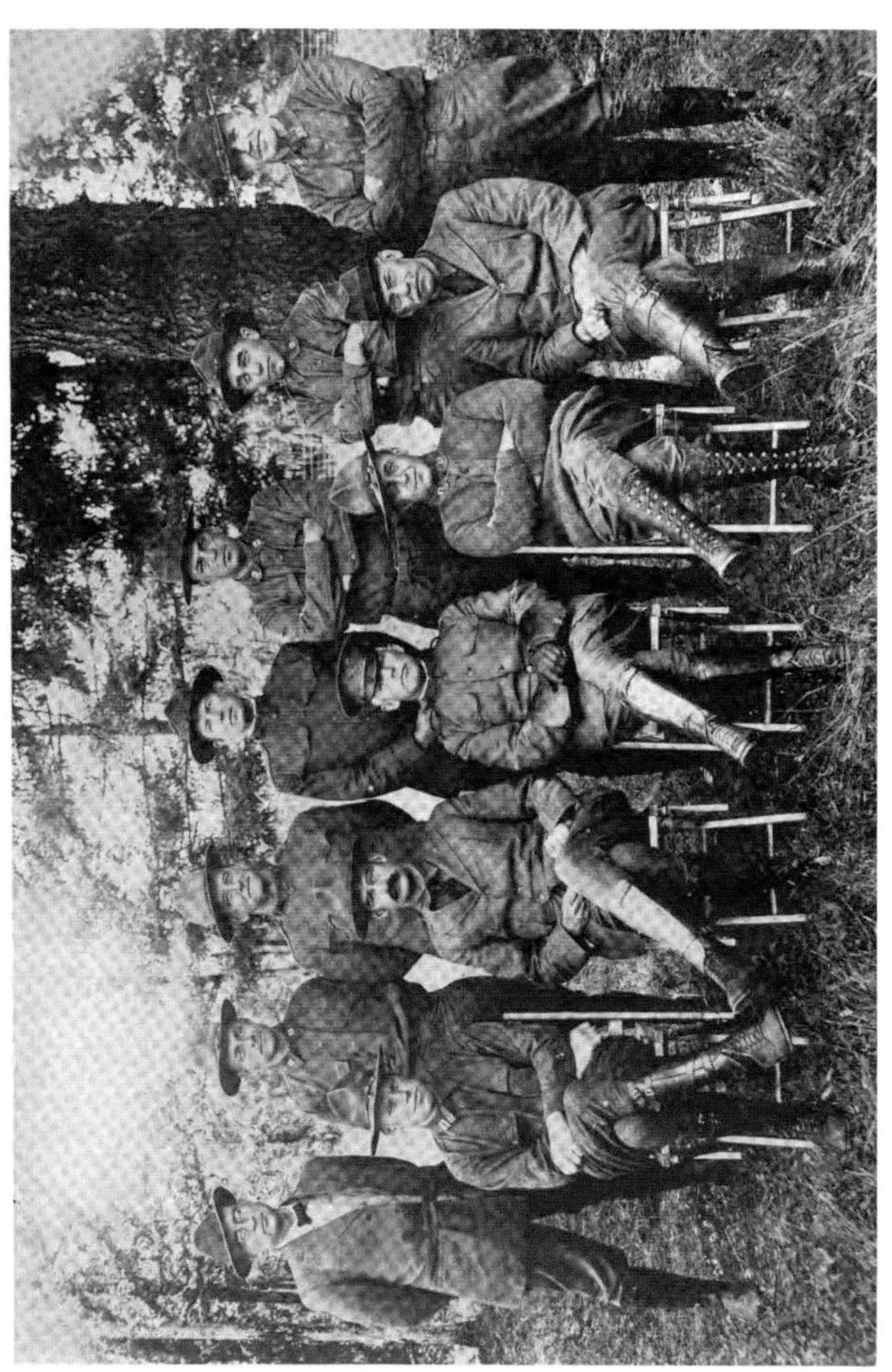

C. L. SMITH   CAPT. PUFFER   CAPT. LANG   CAPT. BRAMLETT   CAPT. HARVEY   CAPT. MacKAY   CAPT. BALL
CAPT. SNYDER   CARL F. PILAT   LT. COL. STONE   CAPT. SMITTEN   CHAS. L. ALDEN

MILITARY ORGANIZATION

Lt. Col. David L. Stone	Constructing Quartermaster
Captain Louis Lang	Assistant to Constructing Quartermaster
Captain H. M. Smitten	Assistant to Constructing Quartermaster
Captain Frost Snyder	Assistant to Constructing Quartermaster
Captain R. M. Bramlett	Assistant to Constructing Quartermaster

CIVILIANS ATTACHED TO MILITARY

Mr. Carl F. Pilat	Town Planner
Mr. Charles H. Alden	Architect and General Superintendent of Buildings
W. J. Roberts	Consulting Engineer Water and Sewers
U. S. Marshall	Engineer of Road Construction

CONTRACTORS' ORGANIZATION

Firms having one-quarter interest each in the contract taken in the name of HURLEY-MASON CO.:

J. E. BONNELL	CORNELL BROTHERS
HURLEY-MASON CO.	TACOMA DREDGING CO.

ADVISORY BOARD

C. B. HURLEY, Chairman

A. F. ALBERTSON	D. I. CORNELL
J. E. BONNELL	G. C. MASON
E. C. CORNELL	EDWARD SIMPSON

(Page Fourteen)

THE SURVEY

The first important step in the construction of Camp Lewis was the completion of a thorough topographic survey of the Nisqually Plain. Here was an area of 140,000 acres that included stretches of dense timber, open wood land, sweeps of prairie, streams, lakes, access to salt water, and a system of roads, railways and street car lines. The problem of so placing the cantonment that most of the natural and artificial advantages might be utilized was a serious one, and it was on the makers of the preliminary survey that the responsibility rested most heavily.

On the third of April, 1917, Captain (now Lieutenant Colonel) A. R. Ehrnbeck and Lieutenants S. L. Scott, C. P. Gross, and F. W. Bonfils, commanding Companies E and F of the Second Regiment, United States Engineers, arrived at Camp Lewis, and in less than a week the work was well under way. Of late the American people have awakened to the fact that the United States Engineers represent the highest type of efficiency and the manner in which its representatives have handled the problem offered by Camp Lewis adds another laurel to its long list of splendid successes.

Two sites were tentatively selected and were ordered investigated by the Headquarters of the Western Department; one being the plain north of American and Sequalitchew Lakes, the other a plain that stretches eastward from the station at Dupont, on the south side of American Lake.

On one of his early visits to the Nisqually Plain, General Bell had been much impressed with the scenic beauty and military possibilities of the open country lying north of American Lake, and the original orders from the War Department were to the effect that the cantonment should be erected on this site. After completing his survey, however, Lieutenant-Colonel Ehrenbeck found that the Dupont, or "Southern," site offered the best facilities and recommended it for the cantonment site in his report.

On May 26th, 1917, Captain (now Lieutenant-Colonel) David L. Stone, Q. M. C., with his staff arrived at Camp Lewis for the purpose of beginning the actual construction work. After inspecting the two proposed sites he recognized the superior advantages of the southern site from the viewpoint of transportation, expansion and maneuver facilities and telegraphed his recommendation to General Liggat, commanding the Western Department, thus opening a question that was supposed to be closed. The merits of the two sites were then carefully compared with the result that the Government definitely selected the southern site.

The plans sent out from the office of the Quartermaster General at Washington, D. C., gave a typical arrangement for an ideal cantonment. It became necessary, therefore, to fit these plans to the selected site; in fact to lay out the cantonment city in such a manner as to best suit the site and serve its military purposes.

At the beginning, when Camp Lewis was but little more than an idea, it was determined by the engineers in charge that in order to prosecute the work with speed and precision, some system of base line measurements had to be adopted.

After a close inspection of the maps of the locality the magnitude of the work was seen and it became evident that the only way to accomplish this result would be to use the railroad surveys for the purpose.

With this in mind a trial survey was projected upon the topographic maps of the section to determine the lines best suited to the ground and at a minimum of cost, such lines being laid so that all the military advantages of the ground were preserved. When this trial work was completed, it was at once seen that in order to make use of the ground to the best the cantonment had to be divided into two parts.

In order to solve the difficult problem, Lt. Colonel Ehrnbeck and Captain Smith devised an ingenious plan: squares of paper were taken and trimmed to scale so as to represent in shape and size units such as Brigades of Infantry, Artillery, et cetera. These were placed on a large map of the area, scaled to 200 feet to the inch and shifted about, arranged and rearranged with much discussion, and finally fixed into place with a view to possible changes.

The stretch of prairie selected for the site is about a mile wide and runs generally in an east and west direction. It is bounded on the north and south sides by a low line of hills. The placing of each half of the cantonment at the base of these hills gave a most ideal arrangement to the military units and left a parade between of splendid proportions. This also agreed with the railroad lines contemplated. Accordingly, on the 5th of July the surveyors started to work.

Taking off from the Northern Pacific Railway Company's yard just below the little station of Dupont, since renamed American Lake, two long curves were run across the Pacific Highway, meeting in a common point. From this point one line continued in an easterly direction following the base of the southern hills for two and one-half miles. The other line continued on a curve to the north until the other line of hills was reached whence it changed its direction and followed the same general easterly course for a like distance.

The cantonment was laid out in the general shape of a horse shoe with its free end bent backward and each leg was served with a single line of railway tracks and a double line of wagon roads.

Locations were made from the paper location of the Railroad lines and distances, directions, and angles were computed. The Survey of the railroad lines was then made on the ground and the map was found to be so accurate that only slight change was necessary in the placing of the entire cantonment.

Upon these two lines the limits of the military organizations were marked by means of a white flag. With these points in the railroad lines to start from, the outside corners of all brigading organizations were established by means of right angled measurements therefrom. These definitely marked the area to be occupied by each different brigade.

From here on the work of marking the buildings on the ground progressed rapidly. The number of field engineer parties was increased from two to four, one two taking the north side and two the south. The center lines of all road crossings and company streets were then established upon the center lines of the railrods and between these the outside limits of each tier of buildings was set off. The length of the buildings now being laid off in the base line, it remained to carry out these lines toward the parade a sufficient distance to insure the proper spacing of all structures.

By this method it was a comparatively easy task for the twenty-four men comprising the field parties to keep well ahead of the ever increasing force of workmen.

This force was being augmented all the time until it finally reached a total of nearly ten thousand men. Great credit is due to the young men comprising the personnel of the field parties. They were fully alive to the necessity of teamwork and co-operation, realizing that if at any time they were caught by the building men, hopeless confusion and delay would result. Speed and accuracy were the watchwords, with the understanding that no matter what problems arose during the course of the work, delays were absolutely taboo.

As a commentary, it is noteworthy that the officials of Camp Lewis were able by the 18th day of September to receive and care for the full complement of officers, and shortly thereafter nearly fifty percent. of the National Army men assigned to the 91st Division.

ADMINISTRATION

HURLEY - MASON COMPANY was represented by MR. C. B. HURLEY and MR. GEORGE C. MASON, its President and Vice President, respectively, who were in direct supervision of the organization and general administration; in direct contact with the office of the Constructing Quartermaster of the Army from whom were received all orders and instructions, such orders being assigned by this office to the departments concerned; also supervising housing and "First Aid to Injured" provisions for the construction forces.

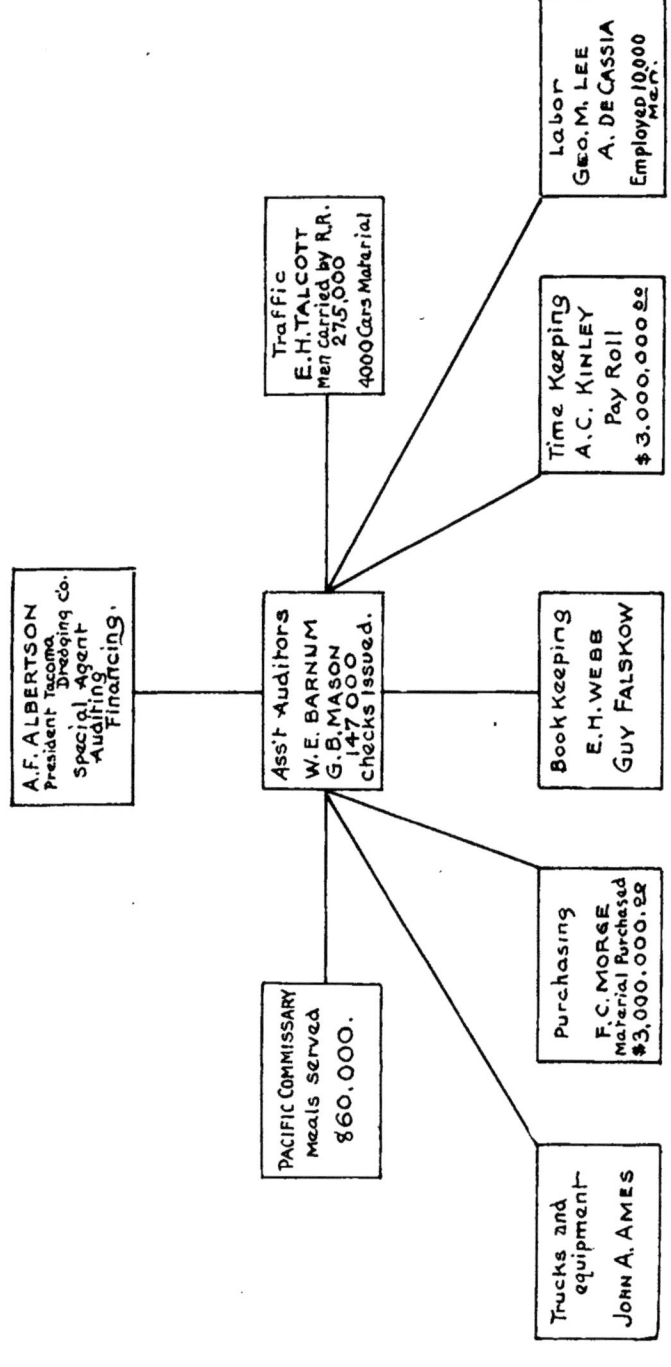

BUILDINGS

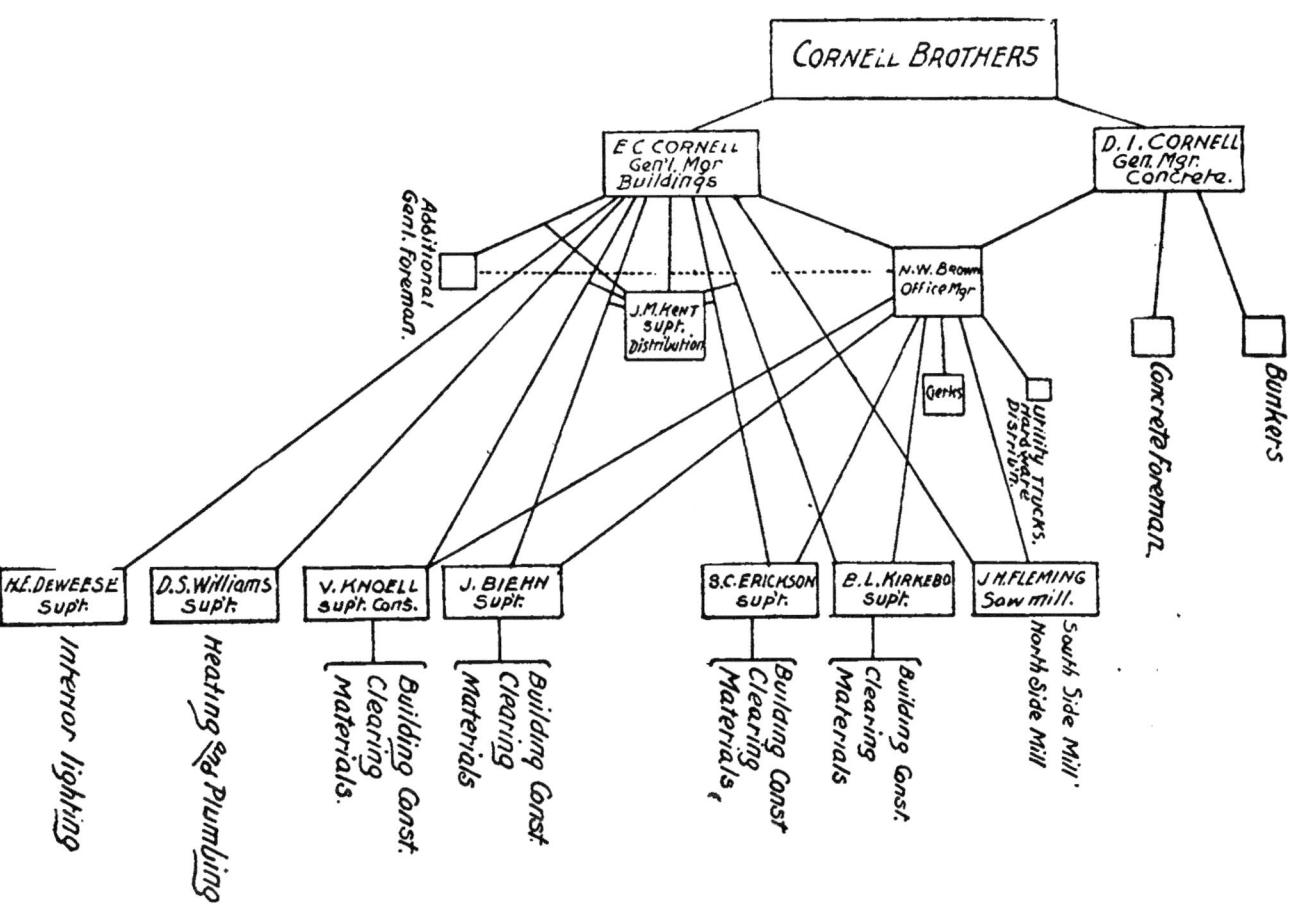

In the formation of the company for the constructing of the CAMP LEWIS CANTONMENT, it fell to the lot of CORNELL BROTHERS to take charge of all building operations in connection with this huge undertaking, namely, providing accommodations for 50,000 men in sixty days.

If one were to stop and think what it must mean to construct a miniature city of some 1863 buildings; of the vast amount of detail involved; of the material to receive and distribute, and of the thousand and one other matters which enter in, one will get a faint idea of the work which fell to the lot of the building department.

It was on Monday morning, the twenty-fifth of June, that a small group of workmen landed at Dupont and was immediately set to work getting ready to start the first building of the cantonment. This building is the one now occupied by the Camp Quartermaster and his staff. A little later in the day two warehouses were gotten under way. During this time and for several days later all the lumber used was brought in by government trucks. By Thursday the first building was ready for occupancy and a portion of the office force was moved to it from Tacoma and two of the warehouses were practically completed.

The first group of barrack buildings, the buildings that were to house the National Army, were commenced on Monday, July second, with about one hundred men. Tehre were thirty-six buildings 43 x 140 feet in the first layout. These were to be used temporarily as bunk-houses for the workmen and are now part of the Second Infantry Brigade. Within ten days a sufficient number of buildings was completed to house the workmen then working, who totaled about 1,080 men, and from this time on men were added as fast as the material arrived.

The tenth of July saw the beginning of construction of the Third Infantry Brigade. Buildings began to loom up over night, as it seemed, and what was once a barren prairie began to take on the appearance of a village.

FIRST BRIGADE

SECOND BRIGADE

THIRD BRIGADE

FOURTH BRIGADE

CONSTRUCTION PROGRESS
August 2nd, 1917

CONSTRUCTION PROGRESS
August 10th, 1917

On the thirteenth of July, another division was begun which was designated as the First Infantry Brigade and joined the work under progress of construction.

By this time lumber was coming in much larger quantities by train and was being distributed as rapidly as it arrived.

It was not until the twenty-third of July that work was started on the Fourth Infantry Brigade.

Three other divisions were later started, known as the Heavy Artillery, the Light Artillery and the Engineers Train.

By August first all divisions were well started with an organization that could handle all of the material that could be delivered by the combined mills of the Northwest.

Lumber arrived in great quantities, as many as seventy cars per day, and it became a matter of balancing the labor to fit the lumber supply.

The method of construction followed on most of the buildings was what might be termed the "knock-down-house" plan.

Two saw-mill plants of eight machines each were installed; one on the north side and one on the south side. The material was cut in these plants according to blue-prints, numbered and delivered to the building for which it was intended; the superintendent or foreman receiving a copy of the blue-print showing the location of each piece delivered. This method of construction made it possible to use rough carpenters with good results.

These plants were run with double shifts and thus were able to keep the building supplied. Small as they were, they were capable of turning out from 150,000 to 200,000 feet per day of eight hours.

The elements favored the rapid completion of the work, as for two months and more no rain fell or at least none in such quantity as to retard the work.

BARRACK'S DORMITORY

BARRACK'S KITCHEN

INTERIOR LIGHTING

Some interesting facts confront us when we turn to the problem of lighting Camp Lewis. About 2,000,000 feet, or 379 miles, of rubber covered copper wire was necessary to wire the 1863 buildings. This wire which carries the current to some 70,000 lamps is supported by porcelain cleats mounted upon 1 x 4-inch wooden running boards. Over 400,000 pairs of cleats and 900,000 8-inch screws were used in this work. One million lineal feet of 1 x 4-inch timber was used to carry the wires and guard them.

Two million, eight hundred thousand wattsof electrical energy, or in other words, 3,753 horse power is used in illuminating the 70,000 lamps.

Each and every building in the cantonment has its individual lighting system, composed of service wires, center of distribution, and branch circuits on which are grouped the lights.

Each service is projected by a main switch and fuse, as is each circuit which has its individual switch and fuses.

Every building from the administration building to the smallest stable in the far away remount station is lighted by electricity.

The usefulness of electricity does not end at the lighting. Every drop of water used is pumped by electrically driven pumps; every loaf of bread is mixed by electric dough mixers; and, in that wonderful institution, the Base Hospital, electricity again plays a most important role. Over 1,400 lights are necessary to illuminate the 70 units which form the complete hospital. All the wires in these buildings are concealed in the walls and attics. The sterilizers of all surgical instruments, running of dental motors, X-Ray machines and lighting of the operating rooms is made simple by the abundant use of electrical energy.

The two miles of connecting corridors which link the many wards into one unit are brilliantly lighted, which makes it possible to move a patient from one of the remote wards to the operating rooms as quickly in the night time as by day.

The work, whch was directed by Mr. H. F. Deweese, assisted by Jack Annis and James Nolan, was organized in such a way as to produce a maximum of speed with a minimum of labor.

Two men and a helper would begin to wire a building and move on to the next one in the same row. They would be followed by others, who ran the service wires and installed the centers of distribution. These, in turn, would be followed by the men who installed the "drops" and ceiling receptacles. Specialization was the prime factor in the great work and the result was a complete and gratifying success.

Camp Buildings

ADMINISTRATION BUILDING

TYPE OF Y. M. C. A. BUILDINGS

CAMP THEATRE

CAMP LIBRARY

KNIGHTS OF COLUMBUS BUILDING

BUILDING SCENE

PLUMBING SYSTEM

The plumbing work at Camp Lewis is one of the largest pieces of work of its sort on the Coast and upon its proper installation depends to a great extent the health of the camp. The camp is provided with 4000 water closets, of the latest vitreous enameled bowl and tanks, six thousand feet of wash troughs fitted with eight thousand five hundred hot and cold faucets, nine hundred urinals, three thousand shower baths, eight hundred and fifty hot water boilers ranging from thirty to seven hundred and sixty gallons in capacity, six hundred and fifty kitchen sinks, seven thousand two hundred brass valves. Sixteen miles of hot and cold water piper, two miles of soil pipe and many thousands of fittings.

Each two hundred-man barrack is provided with two kitchen ranges, two sinks and hot water boiler; and has a separate toilet room 21 x 56 feet long, heated with two large cast iron heaters, and is well ventilated and provided with twelve toilets and ten shower baths fitted with hot and cold water, hot water being supplied by a 760-gallon tank and a large hot water heater. For washing and shaving two long wash troughs are installed and are fitted with hot and cold water. All officers' quarters are provided with separate toilet rooms and bath rooms. The toilet rooms are the same as those of the men, but smaller and contain a steam heater used to heat the quarters.

The Base Hospital group of buildings have a total of six hundred and fifty fixtures, all of the best type of hospital fixtures obtainable. Everything in the plumbing line is the most sanitary that is possible to be obtained. All other buildings include comfort stations for both men and women—Y. M. C. A. buildings, Y. W. C. A. buildings, Knights of Columbus building, officers' and others are all fitted with the best of plumbing.

This work was done under the supervision of D. S. Williams, of Portland, Oregon.

TYPE OF BASE HOSPITAL BUILDINGS

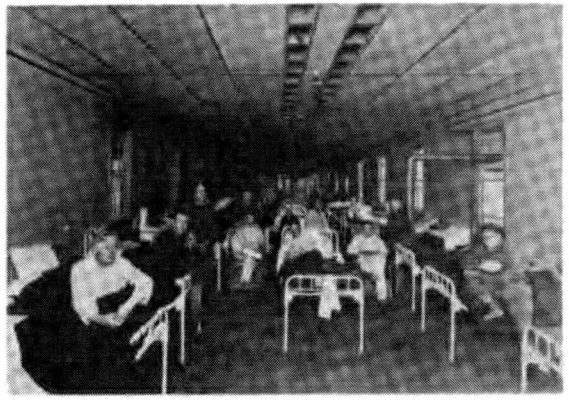

HOSPITAL WARD

ISOLATION WARD

HEATING SYSTEM

The Base Hospital, all Officers' quarters, Regimental Medical Buildings, or Infirmaries, are heated by steam. The balance of the buildings, Barracks, Administrative Buildings, et cetera, are heated by stoves.

The various buildings in the Base Hospital are heated from a central plant, located adjacent to the railroad spur and about the center of the district to be served. The group consists of seventy-four buildings, mostly hospital wards. The wards are all connected by covered corridors, which lend themselves readily to the carrying of the steam mains.

The boiler plant consists of six 150-h. p. boilers with space provided for two additional units.

Coal is the fuel used, and a conveyor elevates it from a pit under the railroad track to a horizontal conveyor over the center of the storage base immediately in front of the boilers. Firing is done by hand direct from the storage bins.

The boilers used for heating carry about ten pounds pressure. One unit carries one hundred and seventy-five pounds pressure to supply high pressure steam to the hospital operating room and laboratory for sterilizing, et cetera, and supplies steam for the hospital laundry.

Hot water for the various buildings is supplied by a hot water circulating system, and is heated at the central plant by a fourteen hundred-gallon Patterson combination heater and hot water storage tank kept circulating by an electrically-driven direct connected three-inch Hill pump with a capacity of two hundred and fifty gallons per minute.

For the heating of these buildings 1,946 radiators are required, with 66,443 square feet of radiation; on the ordinary proportion of radiation to cubic space, the amount of radiation would heat a building four stories high 100 feet wide and four blocks long, assuming four hundred feet to the block.

The heating installation required 4,486 feet of low pressure main, 5,795 feet of main in the corridors—and a total of all sizes and classes of twelve miles of pipe.

The central heating for the Base Hospital was done under a sub-contract by The American District Steam Company, North Tonewanda, New York; E. L. Barnes, Western Manager, and A. W. Peters, Constructing Superintendent.

With a very few exceptions the officers' quarters and administration buildings are heated by individual plants located in a small building adjacent to the quarters.

In most instances the radiation is hung on the wall three feet above the floor, in accordance with the plan of the War Department, and avoids the necessity of placing the boiler in a deep pit.

One hundred and thirty-two boiler plants were required for heating one hundred and forty-four buildings, which required sixteen miles of steel pope and 74,700 square feet of radiation.

The Base Hospital, Officers' Quarters and other buildings heated by steam required in all about 500 tons of radiation and 28 miles of pipe of all sizes. The smokestacks for the individual plants made from galvanized iron would, if set end to end, be one-third as high as Mount Tacoma.

To supply and install ranges, heating stoves and accessories was in itself a sizable task, requiring 900 cooking ranges. For furnishing heat to the barracks, 1,600 wood and coal-burning furnaces were installed, in addition to 1,200 air-tight heaters of smaller dimensions for orderly rooms, officers' quarters and bathrooms.

Incidental to the foregoing, 40,000 feet (40 tons) of sheet iron stove pipe were required. Additional to these figures are 3,200 galvanized iron smokestacks of various lengths and diameters; 2,200 terra cotta, fire-proof tiles and five tons of galvanized iron deflector plates.

Other figures from this same department are interesting. If the galvanized iron vent pipes through which kitchen fumes pass out of the barracks were placed end to end, the stack would be nearly five miles high. The galvanized iron wash troughs total 16,000 feet,—140 tons. Three tons of steel wire were uesd to support smokestacks. Enough asbestos to cover nearly an acre was placed around stoves and ranges for fire protection. The quantity of solder used for the installations enumerated was approximately 30,000 pounds.

All stoves were installed under Lieutenant Graham, working directly under Captain Long.

WATER AND SEWER SYSTEM

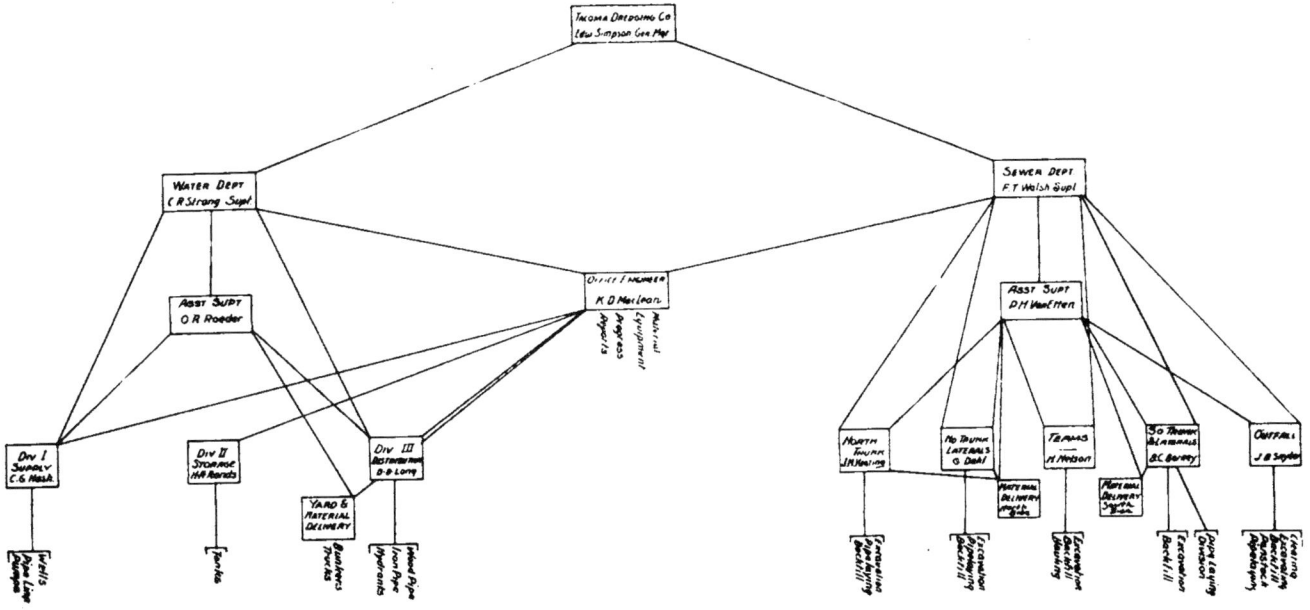

WATER

When we realize that a city is a camp magnified a thousand fold, we can begin to appreciate the responsibility that rested on the men who undertook to supply Camp Lewis with water.

The first step in this important work was taken in the early part of June, 1917. After a serious study of the question it was found that the most promising water supply was offered by some large springs that were situated at the eastern end of Sequalitchew Lake, a clear body of water lying west of American Lake. On being tested the springs showed a flow of two million gallons per day, but as there was no way of ascertaining whether the flow would be continuous it was decided to prospect for wells between American and Sequalitchew Lakes, and samples of the water as found were taken and analyzed for their bacteriological and mineral contents. These analyses proved the remarkable purity of the water, as the samples contained an even lower bacteriological count than that found in ordinary distilled water.

Situated about midway between the springs and the cantonment site is a hill that rises one hundred and thirty-five feet above the surrounding country, which was selected as a reservoir site, and on the 18th day of June, the work of clearing this elevation and the construction of a wagon road connecting this site with the Pacific Highway was commenced.

On June 22nd, a 3-stage 4-inch centrifugal pump was ordered for immediate delivery, and preparations were made for its installation at a battery of wells, consisting of eight 2-inch points

WATER CAMP NO. 1

driven into the ground and connected to a common 6-inch suction pipe. This unit discharged through a 6-inch wooden pipe into a 1500-gallon storage tank installed on Reservoir Hill, and on July 10th the temporary system was placed in service and water was distributed to the construction camp sites through 6-inch and 2-inch mains.

Delivery of materials for the permanent installations was begun on July 15th and with a few exceptions no especial difficulties were encountered in getting sufficient materials to keep the construction forces busy up to the completion of the work.

The accompanying chart shows the progress of various phases of the work. No serious labor difficulties were encountered.

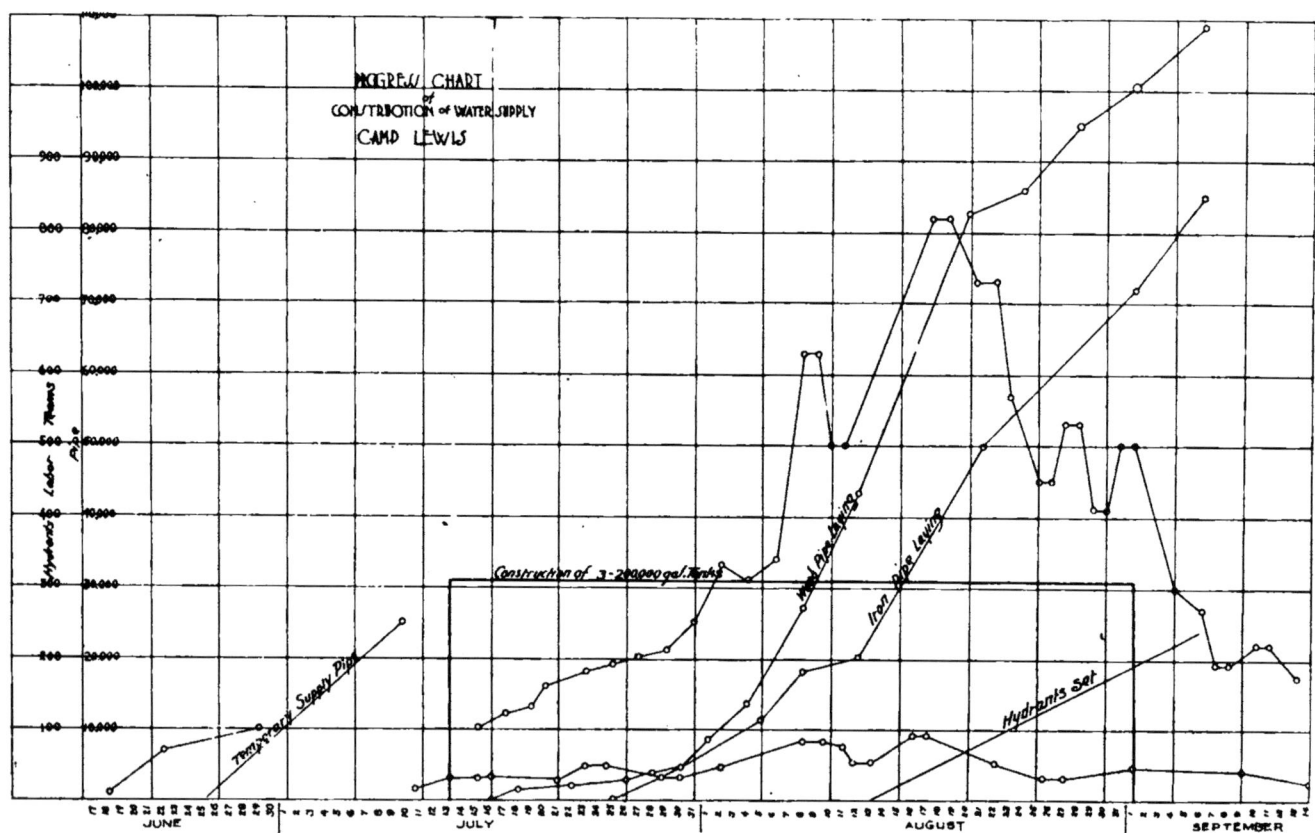

The trenches were all dug by teams with slip scraper and by pick and shovel. The wood pipe used was all machine-banded and was driven by hand-swung rams.

As soon as possible after the completion of any section of wood pipe it was filled with water from the temporary source and tested to its full head capacity and immediately thereafter house connections were changed from the temporary to the permanent lines, and new permanent connections made. It was in these operations that the greatest difficulties of the work were experienced, i. e., in transferring from temporary to permanent service without loss of effective operation; as the plans for the material ordered embraced the use of all the temporary pipe lines in the permanent service and these were laid at a time when the locations were not determined, it was necessary to remove and relay all temporary lines to complete the permanent system.

The permanent water supply has two sources:

1—Well No. 1: The site of the former temporary source is in a depression, whose surface elevation approximates that of Lake Sequalitchew and lies between American and Sequalitchew Lakes.

This site was developed by driving eight 24-foot sections of 4-inch heavy perforated hydraulic pipe into the gravel and connecting these pipes to a common 8-inch suction pipe, which is connected to a 6-inch 2-stage centrifugal pump direct connected to 100-h. p. pump motor.

2—Sequalitchew Springs are located on the side of Sequalitchew Lake adjoining American Lake, which has a surface elevation of 25 feet above Sequalitchew. A dam of gravel excavated from these springs was built around them excluding their discharged water from the Lake and impounding this spring water in a reservoir approximating 75 feet by 100 feet by 6 feet with a concrete overflow spillway to the lake.

Two 6-inch motor driven 2-stage centrifugal pumps and one 6-inch 3-stage centrifugal pump are located at this source.

PUMP STATION AT SEQUALITCHEW SPRINGS

All pumping units discharge into two 12-inch mains which discharge into three 200,000-gallon wooden tanks located on Reservoir Hill. From these tanks the water is distributed through a grid-iron system to all parts of the Camp, starting from the tanks with two 14-inch lines and gradually down to 6-inch pipes. This arrangement is deemed sufficient to supply an ample quantity of water, and to furnish additional insurance of supply in case of accident to any line. This plan is carried throughout the cantonment, practically all lines being in pairs, one at each side of each cantonment leg, but within fire hose reach of each other.

The iron pipe laying was all handled from a centrally located pipe shop, where all stock was inventoried and checked in and out. Five wagons were fitted out with complete pipe threading and cutting facilities and with racks to carry supplies sufficient for one day's work for a crew. Each wagon was fitted out each day with the particular supplies made up from a list made by the general foreman and sent out to its particular job with the necessary quota of men.

In conjunction with them, graphic estimates were made of the work to be done, and each day's work was platted on tracing cloth to the same scale as the estimate and at the end of each day the exact status of each feature of the work was ascertained by an inspection of the progress sheet as compared with the estimate sheet.

600,000-GALLON STORAGE TANKS

These are the facts compiled from the reports of the different engineers who contributed to the success of this vital part of the preparation of Camp Lewis. Briefly stated it means that in a period of seventy days an area of wild land was equipped with a complete water system supplying a city prepared for fifty thousand inhabitants.

SEQUALITCHEW SPRINGS

SEWER SYSTEM

The only features of special interest in the Camp Lewis Sewer System are the magnitude of the job and the limited time in which it was installed. The system was designed for a contonment of roughly 46,000 men, the discharge being in the waters of Puget Sound. The general outline of this system may be compared to a tree. What is referred to as the outfall sewer representing the trunk, the north and south trunk representing a fork in the main body of the tree, and the numerous laterals representing the branches and limbs, making in all a total of 25 miles of sewer.

The outfall, three miles in length, is constructed of 24 and 30-inch pipe, the 30-inch pipe being used where the topography of the country required the minimum grades.

The sewer system was projected upon preliminary topographical maps. Two locations for the outfall sewer were given serious consideration, the first down Sequalitchew Creek, the other west of the Dupont Powder Company's enclosure. The latter location was finally adopted on June 30th, and within a few hours several truck loads of lumber and fifty men were on the job constructing Camp One, which was located about midway on the line of the outfall sewer, from which all the construction of this section was done. But 1,300 feet of 24 and 30-inch sewer pipe were available within reach of this work at the time of starting construction, and it was necessary to have the balance manufactured. Cement pipe was selected and two companies immediately began its manufacture, working 24 hours per day. The first of the newly manufactured pipe was not delivered on the ground until about July 23rd, and thereafter delivery was made at the same rate at which the pipe had been manufactured; the pipe laying crews keeping up with the delivery, so close in fact that eleven extra joints over and above that required for the outfall sewer had not been unloaded from the trucks before the last piece required had been placed in the sewer line.

Camp Lewis is located on a plane about 200 feet above tidewater, which extends to a bluff at the edge of the water.

The sewer work was divided into three sections; the outfall sewer referred to above, the north trunk and north trunk laterals and the south trunk and the south trunk laterals.

Work on the north trunk and north trunk laterals was delayed until after the completion of the first barracks buildings, as they were to be used as camps for the laborers for this and other work.

Final location of the sewer line could not be made until the buildings to be served by the north trunk were definitely located. This work was crowded as fast as possible by the Engineering Department and a location was made for the north trunk so that work started on July 13th. Excavation progressed for about a week before the grades were finally established. The indications were that this north trunk sewer would be quite deep and on account of the uncertainty of the actual depth it was necessary that the trench be started with the expectation of using timber for shoring. About one-half mile of trench had been opened up before the grade was finally established and it was necessary that the same timbering plan be carried to grade on this section. After the grades were finally determ- 11 feet, teams and slip scrapers were used to ex-

CONSTRUCTION OF SEWER LINE

ined and it was found that the cuts did not exceed cavate the top 3½ or 4 feet, the balance being taken out by hand. This plan materially expedited the work and reduced the cost. Work on the north laterals was started as soon as staked, which was July 24th, and all finished on August 25th.

The location of the buildings on the south trunk was not definitely established until July 30th. Work began on this section within 48 hours and the laterals were ready for the excavating crews August 5th. This end of the work, on account of the delay in starting, represented one of the biggest problems encountered, as there were 45,000 feet of pipe to be laid before the 1st of September, which, however,

was completed on the 25th of August, making an average of 1,800 feet per day.

The total sewer to be installed by September 1st amounted to 25 miles. The first piece of sewer pipe was laid July 12th, and the last piece August 25th. As work was carried on on two Sundays, this gave 40 working days, during which time an average of 3,300 feet of pipe per day were laid. From August 7th, the time when work was well started on all the different ends of the job, the average sewer constructed per day amounting to little over 5,000 feet, or practically a mile. The best single day's work was 7,400 feet.

All trenching was done with pick and shovel. Trenching machines of various types were con-

sidered but the character of the soil being loose gravel of graduated size from coarse sand to boulders of one cubic foot did not lend itself to machine handling.

The class of labor obtainable was not particularly familiar with sewer construction, but it proved more efficient than would be expected. Many men from the logging camps were employed who were used to a hard, severe class of labor, and each turned out a full conscientious day's work; in shallow trenches doing equally well as regular sewer men, and in the deep trenches making up for any lack in skill by a willingness to cast out of an eleven-foot trench without complaint.

All crews worked eight hours, no overtime, and but two Sundays. During July, the average number of men employed was 175. During the first half of August, 750, and the last half of August, 950.

POWER SYSTEM

On June 29th a consultation was held between Major David L. Stone, Constructing Quartermaster, American Lake Cantonment, Engineering Corps Officers and officials of the Puget Sound Traction, Light and Power Company to discuss the light and power supply to the American Lake Cantonment.

The Power Company agreed to supply a sufficient amount of current during the construction period from its existing 13,000 volt lines, and to immediately begin the construction of a necessary 50,000 volt transmission line and reconstruction of certain of its 13,000 volt transmission lines to supply power up to the full requirements of the Government,—the supply to be ready by the time the Cantonment was ready for occupancy.

It was further agreed upon that the Power Company would undertake to construct the entire distributing system within the Cantonment, extend for the Government its transmission line to a substation and install the necessary transformers and switching apparatus within the substation.

In order to furnish light and power for the constructing contractors, transformers and services were installed for their office buildings, bunk houses, sawmill and pumping plant. These installations were completed on July 7th.

The placing of orders and the beginning of the construction of the distributing system was somewhat delayed pending the arrival of specifications from Washington. These were on or about July 20th. Orders for material were immediatly placed and construction work was begun August 5th.

The entire work, including the setting of poles, stringing of wires, hanging of transformers, running of services and installation of street lighting system, was completed on October 1st.

Following is a general outline of the amount of material used and work performed:

Total length of wire used (weighing 55 tons) miles 165
Total number of poles set 1,483
Total number of transformers hung:
    Distributing transformers 106
    Street Light transformers 11
Total number of street lights 338
Maximum number of men employed 140

The main step-down transformer station consists of concrete and brick building, approximately 25 feet square, in which are installed two 500 Kw. three phase, 50000/2300 volt self-cooled transformers, together with 50,000 volt disconnecting and oil switches. Three circuits leave this building,—two lighting and miscellaneous small power feeders and one a feeder supplying the pumps. These are controlled from three switch-board panels equipped with oil switches, disconnecting switches, instruments, etc. In the installation of the apparatus in this substation the Power Company's standards were adhered to. Immediately outside of the building there is installed 50,000 volt electrolytic lightning arrester equipment.

On August 1st the Power Company began the construction of 14.7 miles of 50,000 volt transmission line, and the reconstruction of 10.75 miles of existing 13,000 volt transmission line, the stringing of 8.3 miles of 13,000 volt circuit to serve existing customers of the Power Company, the installation of three 375 K. V. A. 50000/2300 volt transformers to replace existing 13,000 volt transformers, and the installation of two 50,000 volt outdoor switching stations. The completion of this work was somewhat delayed by inability to get transmission line material, transformers and switching apparatus. The new transmission lines and permanent transformer station at the Camp were placed in service on October 23rd.

As the Power Company was delayed in placing its new transmission system in service, due to the delay in getting material, and also as there was delay in completing the permanent transformer station, a temporary transformer station was installed with 180 Kw. transformers,—these being served from the existing 13,000-volt lines of the Power Company. This station served the cantonment up to October 23rd, and although the transformers carried at times three times their rated load, no interruption in power service took place.

REMOUNT STATION

AMMUNITION AND SUPPLY TRAIN

RAILROADS

In the chapter on Surveying, we have shown that the location of Camp Lewis was dependent on transportation facilities. When we realize that up to September 4th, 1917, the contractors had used nine thousand five hundred and sixty-five kegs of nails, we can begin to get a faint idea of the gigantic amount of material that has been assembled at the cantonment site.

The feature that played the most important role in the choice of the present site was its proximity to the Tacoma-Olympia branch of the Northern Pacific Railroad, and the improved Pacific Highway, a magnificent automobile road that paralelled the railway.

The Northern Pacific officials were quick to realize the great importance of the project, and the efficiency and dispatch with which they have carried on their part of the work leaves nothing to be desired.

The plans were approved by Lt. Col. Stone on the 24th of June, and on the same date the warehouses and administration buildings were staked by the Engineers and the construction of the buildings was begun the following morning by the Contractors.

Track construction began on June 27th with the laying of the east switch of the "Wye" track system. A track was laid across the Pacifice Highway crossing and completed in three days and a temporary roadway was maintained while the work was being done.

Track was laid past the admiinstration buildings on July 7th, and to the end of the north line by the night of July 12th; and carload shipments were delivered to the contractors just one week after the construction of the north track had been authorized by Lt. Col. Stone.

Track laying on the south line of the cantonment began on July 14th, and all the main lines with spurs have been open for the receipt of freight since the night of July 21st.

RIFLE RANGES

ROADS

Camp Lewis Cantonment lies adjacent to the improved Pacific Highway, so the road construction necessarily embraced only the building of the communicating roads of the cantonment.

The type of road best suited for the heavy traffic, the congested condition of the route during construction, the consideration of the type of soil upon wihch it was to be built and the amount available for the work made a very difficult problem.

The site of the cantonment is a level plain made up of glacial gravel, hundreds of feet deep. On the surface, plant growth has created a black humus which, together with an extremely fine black lava ash, extending down for a depth of from one to two feet, intermixed with fine gravel in the proportion of thirty-five per cent. of gravel to sixty-five per cent. of fine material, makes a material fit for light traffic road construction but unsuited for the heavy truck traffic of the camp.

The type of road finally adopted for the primary roads was as follows: Four to six inches of top soil was removed by means of a road grader, after which the ground was sprinkled and rolled and thrown open to traffic. This formed a very firm sub-grade. On top of this was spread a ten-inch layer of bank gravel, which was spread with Fresno scrapers and hand rakes, the large rocks being thrown out to the side to be picked up later; after which it was sprinkled and rolled.

Roads were thrown open to traffic for a week, being sprinkled daily and the weak spots repaired, after which it was given a good coating of fuel oil. This type of road will require maintenance, but thus far has proven satisfactory under the volume of traffic, often amounting to one truck every five seconds.

The secondary roads were not graveled, being made of the material in the roadway in the following manner. The top soil for the proper width was removed with a road grader, after which the mixture of gravel and humus was plowed to a depth of a foot or more and thrown up into a crown. It was then wet and rolled and satisfactory results were obtained.

EQUIPMENT: All grading of roads was done with three 80-h. p. tractor road graders. The gravel was loaded at a pit within the cantonment with a one cubic yard steam shovel and hauled into place with twelve end-dump auto trucks and three tractors hauling spreader wagons.

All road work was performed under a separate contract by the Independent Asphalt Paving Company under the supervision of U. S. Marshal of the U. S. Office of Public Roads and Rural Engineering.

Contract for the work was signed on July 5th; graveling was completed September 5th, and entire work cleaned up October 1st.

RIFLE PITS

FIR EMERGENCY COMMITTEE

When the United States Government was formulating plans for the development of its National Army it became apparent that extraordinary measures must be taken to supply the necessary materials for the building of the cantonment for these new troops.

With this necessity in view the Committee on National Defense invited ten representative lumbermen from various districts of the country to confer with them on the available wood product supplies, which would be required in all districts where cantonments were to be built.

J. D. Long and J. T. Gregory of Tacoma were appointed on the committee to represent the Northwest District and they were called to Washington to sit in conference on this exceedingly important branch of the construction work projected.

While Mr. Long and Mr. Gregory were in Washington, specifications of lumber requirements and prices were fixed to fit the local available supply and when they returned home they were vested with the authority to purchase all lumber for the construction work.

Too much praise cannot be given Mr. Long and Mr. Gregory for the splendid work done in producing the required supplies and their influence was felt not only in the prompt manufacture and delivery of construction lumber but also of all wooden products such as wooden pipes, tanks, sash, doors and windows.

Credit is also due the lumbermen of the Northwest for the unity of purpose directing their afforts to assist our Government in its immense undertakings.

Y. W. C. A. HOSTESS HOUSE

MILITARY AND CIVILIAN STAFF AND CONTRACTORS ORGANIZATION

by

LT. COL. DAVID L. STONE

The building of the Cantonment at American Lake was by no means the work of any one man. The success of the undertaking was due, first to the general spirit of loyalty and patriotism of the people of this section of the country and second to the co-ordinated and combined effort of those officials, civilian and military, who so ably assisted in bringing the task to a successful conclusion.

It is a source of great satisfaction to the writer to know that no honor can be paid to the construction of this Cantonment without honoring these officials whose names appear below.

MILITARY PERSONNEL

Lieutenant Colonel Arthur Ehrnbeck, Corps of Engineers, U. S. A. in charge of military and topographical engineering work, and construction of rifle and machine gun taget ranges. He also assisted in locating site for Cantonment and grouping and arranging the various regiments and brigades comprising the Cantonment.

Captain Louis M. Lang, Q. M. U. S. R. in immediate charge of building constructiou throughout the Cantonment.

Captain Robert M. Bramlett, Q. M. U. S. R. in charge of all finance and property pertaining to the construction work.

Captain H. M. Smitten, in charge of railroad planning and construction and laying out of buildings and construction of Remount Depot.

Captain Will R. White, assistant to Chief Engineer of water and sewer systems.

Captain Frost Snyder, Q. M. U. S. R. executive officer for the Officer in Charge and in charge of all correspondence, records, etc., pertaining to the work.

Assisting Captain Frost Snyder were Sergeant Lynn L. Hoover, chief stenographer, E. M. Sellers and H. M. Hetzler, stenographers and clerks.

Lieutenant Wilfred Lewis, Corps of Engineers, U. S. R. in charge of construction of Base Hospital and Incinerator plant.

Lieutenant Robert J. Graham, in charge of installation of all stoves, ranges, etc., throughout the Cantonment.

Captain W. J. P. Simpson, corps of Engineers, U. S. R., assistant to Chief Engineer of water and sewer systems.

CIVILIAN STAFF

Carl F. Pilat, Landscape Architect in charge of all parks, roads and street improvements in New York City. Mr. Pilat was principal advising and consulting and executive engineer throughout all branches of the work.

W. J. Roberts, Civil Engineer, Chief Engineer of all water and sewer systems and had entire charge of designing, planning and constructing these systems.

H. E. Smith, Field Auditor, in charge of all accounts connected with construction work and of all checking, inspection and acceptance of all material and all timekeeping and estimates, ably assisted by Mr. Edward Thompson. Mr. Smith's work contributed in large part to the harmony and efficiency of our organization.

CONTRACTORS

Hurley-Mason Company, with whom were associated Messrs. E. C. Cornell and D. I. Cornell of Cornell Brothers, and Messrs. Edward Simpson and A. F. Albertson of the Tacoma Dredging Company, and Mr. J. E. Bonnell.

The prosecution of the work to a successful conclusion by the above named gentlemen showed a thorough knowledge of the contracting business and also an executive and administrative ability of the highest order.

As officials of the Tacoma Dredging Company were also two gentlemen who deserve the highest credit, viz.: Mr. C. A. Strong, who was in actual charge of construction of the entire water system, and Mr. F. J. Walsh, who had charge of the building of the sewer system and the successful completion of these systems is largely due to these men.

Each and every man listed above and every person who has labored faithfully for the success of this work may always be conscious of the fact that he has rendered efficient service to his Government in time of war.

Y. W. C. A. HOSTESS HOUSE

INTERESTING FACTS

Camp Lewis is the first donation of its kind in the history of our country.
The donation comprises an area of 140 square miles.
The present camp covers an area of 2,500 acres.

AUDITING DEPARTMENT:

Office employees	160
Material purchased	$3,000,000
Pay roll	3,000,000
Checks issued	147,000
Cars material handled	4,000
Meals served	860,000
Men handled by railroad	275,000

BUILDINGS:

Buildings erected	1,863
Lumber used	53,966,639 ft. B. M.
Nails	614 tons
Roofing paper (1-ply and 2-ply)	435 acres
Sheathing paper	425 acres
Doors	14,567
Window sash	57,417

When construction was under way 11 1/6 barracks 43 ft by 140 ft. and 6 1/5 stables 29 ft. by 140 ft. were built each day of 8 hours.

WATER:

Pipe lines laid	37.1 miles
Maximum pipe lines laid in one day	2.7 miles
Hydrants	249
Wells driven	4
Pumping units installed	4
Tanks erected	3
Capacity of tanks	600,000 gallons

SEWERS:

Pipe laid	28.8 miles
Maximum pipe laid in one day	1.2 miles
Manholes built	136

ELECTRIC POWER AND LIGHTING:

Wire used	703 miles
Poles set	1,483
Transformers set	128
Street lights	376
Lamps	70,000
Porcelain cleats used	400,000
Power utilized	3,750 h. p.

PLUMBING:

Water closets installed	4,000
Urinals	900
Shower baths	3,000
Kitchen sinks	650
Hot water boilers	850
Hot and cold faucets	8,500
Brass valves	7,200
Wash troughs	3 miles
Hot and cold water pipes	16 miles
Soil pipe	2 miles

HEATING:

Boilers installed	138
Radiators	4,900
Furnaces	1,660
Cooking ranges	980
Air-tight stoves	1,430
Pipe	40 miles
Smoke stacks	1.55 miles
Sheet iron stove pipe	8 miles
Solder used	15 tons
Asbestos around stoves	1 acre

RAILROAD:

Main line	6.07 miles
Spurs and sidings	2.28 miles
Spikes used	25.5 miles
Ties	23,500

ROADS:

Gravel macadam	7.5 miles
Rolled and graded	26 miles

Printed by Libri Plureos GmbH in Hamburg, Germany